Enjoying the

PEMBROKESHIRE COAST

Enjoying the PEMBROKESHIRE COAST

ROLY SMITH

HALSGROVE

First published in Great Britain in 2006

Front cover photograph: *Marloes Sands,* by Chris Warren.
Back cover photograph: *The twin hills are prominent features of Ramsey Island, long linked with nearby St Davids,* by Chris Warren.

British Library Cataloguing-in-Publication Data
A CIP record for this title is available from the British Library

ISBN 1 84114 433 9
ISBN 978 1 84114 433 7

HALSGROVE
Halsgrove House
Lower Moor Way
Tiverton, Devon EX16 6SS
Tel: 01884 243242
Fax: 01884 243325
email: sales@halsgrove.com
website: www.halsgrove.com

Printed and bound by D'Auria Industrie Grafiche Spa, Italy

Contents

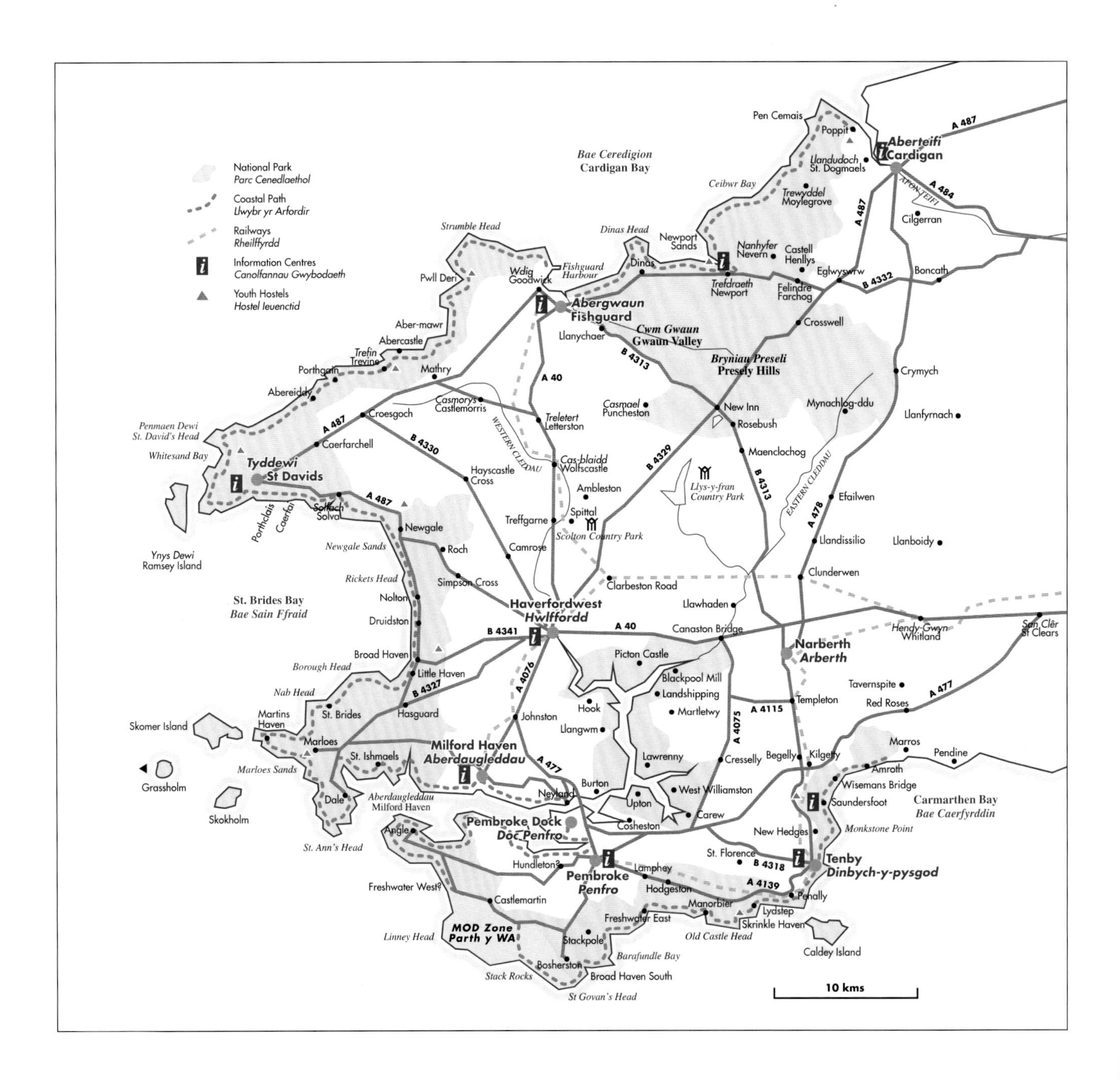

National Park
Parc Cenedlaethol
Coastal Path
Llwybr yr Arfordir
Railways
Rheilffyrdd
Information Centres
Canolfannau Gwybodaeth
Youth Hostels
Hostel Ieuenctid
Bae Ceredigion
Cardigan Bay
Pen Cemais
Poppit
Aberteifi
Cardigan
A 487
Llandudoch
St. Dogmaels
Ceibwr Bay
Trewyddel
Moylegrove
A 484
Afon Teifi
Cilgerran
Strumble Head
Dinas Head
Newport Sands
Nanhyfer
Nevern
Castell Henllys
Eglwyswrw
B 4332
Boncath
Pwll Deri
Wdig
Goodwick
Fishguard Harbour
Dinas
Trefdraeth
Newport
Felindre Farchog
Abergwaun
Fishguard
Crosswell
Aber-mawr
Abercastle
Llanychaer
Cwm Gwaun
Gwaun Valley
Trefin
Trevine
B 4313
Bryniau Preseli
Presely Hills
Porthgain
Mathry
A 40
Crymych
Abereiddy
Casmorys
Castlemorris
Casmael
Puncheston
New Inn
Mynachlog-ddu
Penmaen Dewi
St. David's Head
Croesgoch
Treletert
Letterston
Rosebush
Llanfyrnach
Caerfarchell
B 4330
Western Cleddau
Maenclochog
Whitesand Bay
Tyddewi
St Davids
Hayscastle Cross
Cas-blaidd
Wolfscastle
B 4329
Llys-y-fran Country Park
Eastern Cleddau
Ambleston
Efailwen
A 487
Solfach
Solva
Porthclais
Caerfai
Newgale
Treffgarne
Spittal
Scolton Country Park
A 478
Llandissilio
Llanboidy
Ynys Dewi
Ramsey Island
Newgale Sands
Roch
Camrose
Rickets Head
Simpson Cross
Clarbeston Road
Clunderwen
St. Brides Bay
Bae Sain Ffraid
Nolton
Haverfordwest
Hwlffordd
Llawhaden
Druidston
B 4341
A 40
Canaston Bridge
Narberth
Arberth
Hendy-Gwyn
Whitland
San Clêr
St Clears
Broad Haven
Picton Castle
Borough Head
Little Haven
Blackpool Mill
A 4076
Landshipping
Tavernspite
B 4327
Hook
Martletwy
A 4115
Templeton
Red Roses
A 477
Nab Head
Martins Haven
St. Brides
Hasguard
Johnston
Skomer Island
Llangwm
A 4075
Marloes
Milford Haven
Aberdaugleddau
Marros
St. Ishmaels
Lawrenny
Cresselly
Begelly
Kilgetty
Pendine
A 477
Amroth
Marloes Sands
Grassholm
Burton
West Williamston
Wisemans Bridge
Dale
Aberdaugleddau
Milford Haven
Neyland
Upton
Saundersfoot
Carmarthen Bay
Bae Caerfyrddin
Skokholm
Pembroke Dock
Doc Penfro
Cosheston
Carew
Monkstone Point
Angle
New Hedges
St. Ann's Head
St. Florence
B 4318
Tenby
Dinbych-y-pysgod
Hundleton
Lamphey
Pembroke
Penfro
A 4139
Freshwater West
Hodgeston
Penally
Castlemartin
Manorbier
Lydstep
Freshwater East
Skrinkle Haven
Linney Head
MOD Zone
Parth y WA
Stackpole
Old Castle Head
Caldey Island
Barafundle Bay
Bosherston
Stack Rocks
Broad Haven South
St Govan's Head
10 kms

Foreword

It has been my pleasure and privilege to be Chairman of the Pembrokeshire Coast National Park Authority for three years. And it is my very pleasant duty to welcome you the reader to *Enjoying the Pembrokeshire Coast*. I am sure that this publication will help you to do just that.

The Pembrokeshire Coast is unique among Britain's very special family of National Parks in being the only one which is principally coastal.

Wherever you are in Pembrokeshire you are close to some of the finest coastal scenery in Europe, all ribboned by the superb 186-mile Coast Path, and short boat trips away from world-renowned bird islands.

This National Park also includes the Preseli Hills – magical uplands which are so much a part of British history, and the source of Stonehenge's famous Bluestones. And there is the Daugleddau, the secluded tree-lined inner estuarine reaches around the fiord-like Haven Waterway.

Among many challenges facing us is getting as wide a range of people as possible 'out there' to enjoy the Pembrokeshire Coast National Park. Apart from the Coast Path – one of the UK's National Trails – there are over 600 miles of inland paths to enjoy. Our website features many circular walks – all easily downloadable from home computers – and these include walks for all abilities.

We have always led the way in access and recreation – it was in Pembrokeshire that the concept of 'guided walks' was originally pioneered and developed. And our 'green' transport initiatives are now making a major impact. So, make the most of these services which will help to enhance your experience of this wonderful location.

Our efforts are increasingly focused on engaging with all sections of society by building social inclusion into our mainstream work, as well as leading on sustainability.

Enjoy the Pembrokeshire Coast!

Stephen Watkins
Chairman, Pembrokeshire Coast National Park Authority
March 2006

To the memory of R.M. Lockley,
who introduced this wonderful coast and its wildlife
to so many people through his many books.

Acknowledgements

The author would particularly like to thank his old friend and former colleague, John Evans, Communications Officer of the Pembrokeshire Coast National Park Authority, for his thorough checking of the manuscript; Stephen Watkins, Chairman of the Authority, for his foreword, and all the photographers listed below for the use of their images.

Photographic Acknowledgements

National Park Authority
Pages 10, 11, 12, 13, 14, 15, 16, 18 (bottom), 19 (left), 21, 22, 24, 25, 30 (left), 32, 38, 40, 42, 45 (left), 48 (top left, top right and bottom right), 53, 55, 56, 63, 66, 67, 69, 71, 72, 75 (left), 86

Aurora
Pages 13, 29, 35 (both), 45 (right), 48 (bottom left), P50 (top and left), 68

Chris Warren
Cover plus Pages 17, 19 (lower right), 20, 26, 28, 34, 37, 46, 49, 62, 83 (top)

Gareth Davies
Pages 18 (top), 19 (top right), 30 (right), 31, 36 (top), 41, 44 (both); 50 (right), 54, 61, 70, 74, 75 (right), 77, 78, 79, 80, 81, 83 (left and right)

John Cattini
Page 36 (Caldey Abbey)

Greenways/Pembrokeshire County Council
Pages 60, 64, 65

Janet Baxter
Page 43

The impressive sweep of Whitesands Bay, Carn Llidi in the distance.

1. Introduction

There can be few places in Britain where a description coined a thousand years ago can still be applied today. But the view of Pembrokeshire as *gwlad hud a lledrith* – 'land of mystery and enchantment' – expressed by the anonymous author of *The Mabinogion* in the famous eleventh-century collection of Welsh folk tales and legends, still has not been bettered.

It is a land of sharp contrasts, from dizzying cliffs to secluded, sandy coves on the coast; and from wild, tumuli-studded moorland to deep, oak-fringed estuaries which wind for many miles inland. The landscapes vary from the misty outcrops of the Preseli Hills to the spume-flecked coastline and the mellow, sheltered estuaries of the Daugleddau.

That feeling of mystery and enchantment still hangs in the air above the massive stones of the cromlechs and the walls of the ruined castles and cathedrals of Carew, Pembroke, Manorbier and St Davids, and is echoed by the clouds of screaming seabirds which haunt the many romantic islands guarding the famous coastline.

Once dubbed 'Little England beyond Wales', Pembrokeshire thrusts its rock-clawed fingers out into the storm-wracked Celtic Sea as the last windswept outpost of Wales, and the first landfall for many invaders throughout history, most recently in the last invasion of these islands at Carregwasted Point in 1797.

The Preselis viewed from Rhosfach Common near Mynachlog-ddu.

Gors Fawr, the only circle of free-standing stones in Pembrokeshire.

Giraldus Cambrensis, the proud Welshman who was born to Norman parents at Manorbier Castle on the south coast around 1146, provided another glowing description of his homeland in his *Itinerary through Wales* in 1188. 'Penbroch (Pembroke),' he claimed, 'is the finest part of the province of Demetia. And Demetia (the modern county of Dyfed) is the most beautiful part of Wales.'

Few of the millions of visitors who make the long journey along the M4 and A40 would disagree with that assessment from eight centuries ago. Tenby has been a favourite resort for well over a century, and Pembrokeshire is a popular destination for the people of the cities of South Wales, such as Cardiff and Swansea, as it was for the former coal-mining communities of the Valleys.

So when the Pembrokeshire Coast was designated the fifth UK National Park in 1952, it gave long overdue protection to some of the most beautiful coastline not only in Britain but the whole of Europe. That glorious coastline is threaded by the 186-mile Pembrokeshire Coast National Trail, which opened in 1970, and which is still unquestionably the finest way to get to know the National Park.

To walk the Coast Path in spring or early summer is the most pleasurable assault on the visual and olfactory senses you can have in Britain, and possibly the world. You walk on a carpet of wildflowers – bluebells, red and white campions, ragged robin, thrift, vetches and primroses – which paint the clifftops with an artist's palette of colour. No wonder painters love the Pembrokeshire Coast.

The same floral explosion is witnessed on the islands, especially Skomer, which is transformed into a misty blue and scarlet children's colouring book landscape by the rolling acres of bluebells and campions. As the comical, clown-like puffins swoop in and out of their burrows at your feet, and the grey seals gambol in the crashing seas below, you may be forgiven for thinking that you have already arrived in heaven.

Despite its peaceful appearance today, the history of Pembrokeshire is one of division and strife. When the Normans came and imposed their castles on the landscape, they were deliberately designed to intimidate the native people. And the line of castles they built, stretching from Brandy Brook near Newgale in the west to Amroth in the east, effectively split the county into two – a division which is still recognisable today and marked by the invisible cultural line known as the 'Landsker'.

The viewpoint on Foel Eryr (Eagle's Rock), the second highest point in the Preselis.

To the north of the line, the buildings, language and place names are still very Welsh, and the area is still sometimes known as 'the Welshry'. Churches and chapels have that Spartan Welsh look about them, and coastal headlands are known as *pens* and estuaries have the Welsh prefix *aber*.

The Daugleddau, inner sanctuary of the National Park, seen near Minwear.

To the south, or in the 'Englishry', farms and settlements generally have English-sounding names, the churches have English-looking four-square towers, the bays are 'havens' and headlands become 'points'. While it is quite acceptable now to marry across the Landsker, at one time it was strictly frowned upon and something which seldom occurred, a fact still reflected in the Welsh surnames in the north and English to the south.

While Pembrokeshire is still unquestionably Welsh at heart, its proximity to the ancient trade routes of the Irish Sea and Bristol Channel has always made it more outward-looking than many other counties. That trade may have started with the

Carn Ingli – the Hill of Angels – which overlooks Newport and its bay.

apparent transportation of Stonehenge's inner circle of 80 bluestones, quarried from the Preseli Hills in Neolithic times, perhaps 5000 years ago. The chieftains of the people who lived in those prehistoric times were celebrated in their death by the construction of numerous cromlechs or chambered tombs such as Pentre Ifan and Carreg Samson, now denuded of their earthen covering and looking like gigantic megalithic coffee tables. Certainly, Phoenician merchants from the distant Mediterranean also called at Pembrokeshire 'ports' from Roman times and possibly before.

Later, Nelson's wooden walls used the wonderful natural harbour of Milford Haven, which he thought to be one of the finest deep water harbours in the world. Today, giant supertankers glide in and out of the same harbour, providing constantly changing points of interest to the viewer from the shore.

The Pembrokeshire Coast is the only National Park in Britain to be predominately coastal in character, and at only 240 square miles/620 square km, it is one of the smallest of the family. The tang of the sea is almost always present, because nowhere is more than 10 miles from the ocean. The coastline covers 260 miles, and there are over 50 glorious beaches.

The Pembrokeshire Coast is one of the most densely populated of our National Parks, with around 24,500 residents, a number which is swamped by the estimated five million visitors every year.

But as with any other beautiful area, the visitors tend to congregate around the beauty spots, like bees to honey. If you are prepared and able to walk that extra mile, you will still find that delectable peace and tranquillity which first attracted Geraldus and the writer of *The Mabinogion* ten centuries ago.

Did you know?

Ten fascinating facts about Pembrokeshire

- The Pembrokeshire Coast was the fifth National Park in Britain
- The razorbill which is the Park's emblem is nicknamed 'Reggie'
- St Davids is the smallest city in Britain
- Carew Castle has a ghost – the White Lady – thought to be Nest, wife of Gerald, keeper of Pembroke Castle
- The Skomer Marine Nature Reserve is one of only two in Britain
- Skomer shares the world's largest population of Manx shearwaters
- It also has the largest grey seal colony in southern Britain
- There are 50 beaches, many of which have won European awards for their cleanliness
- The coastline extends for 260 miles – the distance between London and the Lake District
- The oldest Pre-cambrian rocks in the Park are 2000 million years old

Broad Haven South – one of many superb sandy Pembrokeshire beaches.

An iconic image: The Green Bridge of Wales.

2. The South and Daugleddau

The secret, secluded area of the National Park which is centred on the drowned estuaries of the tidal waters of the twin Cleddau rivers and the Carew and the Cresswell tributaries, is referred to by the National Park Authority as its 'inner sanctuary.'

And it's a description which perfectly matches the quiet, richly-wooded stretches of these tranquil rivers which empty into the broad natural harbour formed by Milford Haven. Once a busy commercial waterway taking the products of quarries, collieries, kilns, mills and farms down to Milford Haven and the sea, the Daugleddau is now a quiet backwater mainly frequented by pleasure craft. The high drama of the coastal cliffs seems miles away, and the rivers lie at the heart of an essential, if unheralded, part of the Pembrokeshire scene.

Intimate communities such as Slebech, Minwear, Landshipping, Lawrenny, Llangwm and Carew, with its splendid ruined castle dating from the thirteenth century and associated tidal mill, lie on the estuary banks. Inland is Picton Castle, near Picton Ferry, built by Sir John Wogan in the early fourteenth century and later occupied by Owain Glyndwr.

The romantic ruins of Carew Castle, 'modernised' with mullioned windows by Sir John Perrot in the sixteenth century, and nearby mill are both in the care of the National Park Authority. Close by is the intricately-carved Carew Cross, which commemorates King Maredudd, who died in 1035. Carew's 'French Mill' was until fairly recently one of the few operational tidal mills in the country, and it is also open to the public.

For thirty years the National Park maintained the grounds of Upton Castle – a private residence – near Coheston, where over 250 different species of trees and shrubs clothe the wooded valley which leads down to the Carew River. A charitable trust has taken on this role at Upton.

The southern part of the Park also has more than its fair share of that dramatic coastal scenery for which this National Park is best known. It is particularly well seen in the stretch of the

Elegug Stacks – spectacular limestone features in a dramatic coastline.

Carew Castle – four centuries of living history.

Carew Mill (also known as the French Mill), in the care of the National Park Authority.

coastal path between Linney Head and Manorbier, where limestones from the Carboniferous period meet the sea to create some of the finest coastal scenery in Europe.

Spectacular natural features such as the soaring 'flying buttress' known as the Green Bridge of Wales and the nearby isolated Elegug Stacks on the Castlemartin coast were formed through differential erosion of the limestone, which was also the cause of the many sea caves, blowholes and arches seen along this coast. It is a favourite area for rock climbers, who have cooperated with the Park authorities in restricting their climbing activities during the breeding season of cliff-nesting birds like the peregrine falcon and chough.

Compromise has to be the order of the day in many situations in multi-use countryside such as the National Park. Perhaps the biggest compromise of all is the presence of the Army training ranges at Castlemartin, Penally and Manorbier. The military have been in this part of Pembrokeshire for over fifty years, and access is restricted (see notice boards and the *Coast to Coast* newspaper for details).

Ironically, the exclusion of the public and commercial farming has meant that there has been a bonus for wildlife, and this area of the coast is now home to a range of flora and fauna already lost in other parts of Britain, including bats. A National Park Ranger works with the Ministry of Defence to balance recreation and conservation with the military needs of the area.

Parts of the area are designated Sites of Special Scientific Interest (SSSIs) and European Special Areas of Conservation and Special Protection Areas. The offshore parts of the ranges are also within the Pembrokeshire Marine Special Area of Conservation.

Remains of ancient human history have also been preserved by the absence of intensive farming from the area, and together with several scheduled ancient monuments, extensive medieval field systems have survived on the western range, along with two substantial listed farmsteads at Brownslade and Pricaston. The medieval St Govan's Chapel, former home of an anchorite, is tucked away under the cliffs near Bosherton within the eastern range.

Probably the best, most interesting, and safest way to explore this fascinating area is to join one of the guided walks which the National Park Authority runs throughout the summer. Inland from the coast near St Govan's Chapel are the extensive lily ponds at Bosherston, the home of a variety of water life from iridescent dragonflies and mayflies to the elusive otter. The 80 acres (32 ha) of ponds, noted for the dazzling white blooms of the lilies in early summer, were created as fish ponds by the Earl of Cawdor on his Stackpole Estate in the late

St Govan's Chapel – reached by a flight of steps cut into the cliff.

Bosherston Lily Ponds, crossed by causeways, are the haunt of much wildlife.

eighteenth century, and now constitute the largest area of open fresh water in the National Park.

The largest settlement actually within the National Park is the charming resort of Tenby, clustered around its sheltered harbour, and watched over by the ruins of its castle. Tenby can also boast of being one of the sunniest spots in Wales, a fact appreciated by the thousands of holidaymakers who annually descend on its narrow streets.

Milford Haven land and seascape, from the Cleddau Toll Bridge.

Picture postcard harbour scene at Tenby.

Tenby's past is everywhere to be seen, from the five gates in the mostly intact town walls, which were last strengthened and repaired against the threat of the Spanish Armada in 1588, to the charming but tiny restored Tudor Merchant's House (National Trust) in Bridge Street, which dates from the late fifteenth century.

Other resorts along this sunny coast include Saundersfoot, which started life in the nineteenth century as a coal-exporting port, but which now is a thriving holiday centre; Manorbier, described by Giraldus Cambrensis as 'the most delectable spot in Wales' with its superb Norman castle (where Giraldus was born in 1146) and wonderful beach; Freshwater East; Barafundle; Stackpole and Broad Haven.

Lydstep is another pleasant village whose beautiful beach lies between the headlands of Giltar and Lydstep Head, which is in the care of the National Trust and offers fine views of nearby Caldey Island, the Gower and, on a good day, as far as Lundy Island in the Bristol Channel.

Milford Haven

Lord Horatio Nelson of Trafalgar fame rightly claimed that Milford Haven was one of the finest deep water harbours in the world, and it has attracted seafarers since the days of the Vikings. It has a rich naval tradition, and many of the Royal Navy's 'wooden walls' were built at Pembroke Dock, as were later iron-sided battleships, cruisers and destroyers. It was an important naval and merchant shipping base in both World Wars, and also a base for flying boats during the Battle of the Atlantic. Oil refineries came to Milford Haven in the 1950s and it soon became Britain's biggest oil port. The Haven can accommodate massive tankers of up to 350,000 tonnes in support of its refineries.

Whitesands Bay and Ramsey Island, from the summit of Carn Llidi.

3. The West

With the splendour of late summer
spread out in the land below me
and stillness where the bare crown
was hewn, the grey outcrop,
and my high fortress looking out over the sea
and the waves once more washing over the rocks.

Waldo Williams (1936)

Local poet Waldo Williams' description of the St Davids Peninsula perfectly fits the view from the rocky summit of Carn Llidi, the highest of the three distinctive little volcanic Ordovician peaks which rise spectacularly from the surrounding moorland.

Rising to 594feet/181m above the Pembrokeshire Plain, Carn Llidi commands a wonderful view westwards across the royal-hued heather over Porth Melgan to the rocky spine of St Davids Head, which points unerringly to the isolated crags of the Bishops and Clerks rocks, with the level plateau of Ramsey Island to the south.

On a clear day, you should be able to make out the Wicklow Hills south of Dublin across the Irish Sea, and even the serrated peaks of Snowdonia to the north. Closer at hand, small white-walled farms dot the landscape, with St Davids Youth Hostel at Llaethdy on the foot of the mountain to the south.

In the shallow, secluded valley between the peak and the sea, an extensive field system of small walled enclosures dates back to the Bronze Age, and the lichen-draped, shallow burial chamber of Coetan Arthur out towards St Davids Head perhaps marks the last resting place of one of the leaders of this long-lost community. There are other burial chambers on the summit of Carn Llidi, showing that, even in death, the ancestors watched over their successors.

Beneath Carnedd Lleithr, the second of three peaks of the St Davids peninsula, the crumbling ruins of the former Quaker settlement of Maes-y-Mynydd date back to 1750, but it was depopulated apparently as the result of a poisoned well in 1832.

The third, northernmost peak, the sphinx-like Penberi, commands fine views from its rocky 574ft/175m summit, also known as Kite's Head Rock, especially west towards Carn Llidi and the islands. North from Penberi, the industrial past of Pembrokeshire is evident at places like the tiny ports of Abereiddi, with its famous flooded quarry known as the Blue Lagoon, and Porthgain, where there are the remains of brick-works and slate quarries. Inland from Cwm Badau near Abercastle stands another of Pembrokeshire's famous free-standing cromlechs – Carreg Samson.

To the south of Penberi, the level boggy expanse of Dowrog Common was traditionally common land used by the people of St Davids, but is now managed by the Wildlife Trust, South and West Wales, as a Site of Special Scientific Interest (SSSI). Maen Dewi, the largest and highest (eight feet) standing stone in the area, stands near the isolated cottage of Drws Gobaith, in the centre of the common.

St Davids – cathedral in a valley.

The broad sweep of Marloes Sands.

South of St Davids Head the broad, golden expanse of Whitesands Bay is one of Pembrokeshire's most popular beaches and is the alleged departure point of St Patrick when he first journeyed from Wales to Ireland in the sixth century.

Further south beyond the delightful little harbour village of Solva is Newgale Sands – where a two-mile strip of golden sands is backed by a storm ridge of shingle – Broad Haven and Little Haven, all of which are popular with holidaymakers. Another famous beach on the west coast is Marloes Sands, between the Dale and Marloes peninsulas. Famed for its rocky outcrops like the Three Chimneys rocks, where three ribs of Silurian rock have been thrust into a vertical position by powerful earth movements, Marloes Sands also features Gateholm Island at the western end, which can be reached on foot at low tide.

Martin's Haven, on the Marloes peninsula, is the embarkation point for boat trips to Skomer, Skokholm and distant Grassholm. The headland and promontory Iron Age fort known as the Deer Park overlooks the treacherous rip tide of Jack Sound between the mainland and Skomer.

The prominent lighthouse on St Ann's Head at the southernmost extremity of the Dale peninsula acts as an important guide to the oil tankers and other shipping which constantly ply in and out of Milford Haven.

The west coast also boasts Britain's smallest city – the ancient settlement of St Davids (Ty Ddewi) which lies to the south of Carn Llidi in the valley of the River Alun, dubbed by Giraldus 'the Vale of the Roses'.

Walkers catch their breath overlooking the superb Marloes Sands.

This perfect little cathedral city has been a place of pilgrimage for over eight centuries, and it still exudes that air of sanctity which its namesake saint gave it when he came here in the sixth century. The Normans recognised the power of David's faith, and rebuilt his monastery here as the present, purple sandstone-walled cathedral, which has been extended and added to over the centuries.

As you approach the cathedral from the town, it always comes as a surprise to find it tucked away in a hollow at the bottom of the 39 steps which lead down from the medieval gateway of Porth y Twr. Legend has it that it was built in this low-lying spot to escape the attention of raiding Vikings.

The cathedral interior is breathtaking, with the Gothic arches in the nave leading up (literally, because the cathedral is built on a slope) towards the gloriously ornate stone rood screen which conceals the choir and high altar. Above you is the magnificently carved fifteenth-century oak ceiling, lit by the sunlight which streams in through the medieval plain and stained-glass windows.

Nearby stands the romantic ruins of what was once the Bishop's Palace, built by Henry de Gower in the fourteenth century, a monument to the former importance of the bishopric of St Davids and the rich history of this superb capital city.

Dewi Sant

St David – or Dewi Sant – is the patron saint of Wales, and is inextricably linked with Pembrokeshire and the peninsula where he was born and lived. The story goes that he was born to St Non during a violent storm on the south coast of the peninsula and, as she gave birth, a spring of crystal-clear water burst forth on the spot, which is now known as St Non's Well. David was educated in the ways of the church and as more and more miracles were ascribed to him, the name of St David spread throughout Britain. He returned to Pembrokeshire to build his first church on the slopes of Carn Llidi, but after the foundations were destroyed, an angel is said to have advised him to build it in the valley of the River Alun, where the medieval cathedral of St Davids now stands. After he died, allegedly at the age of 147 in 588, he was buried in his cathedral. St Davids became so important as a place of pilgrimage that two pilgrimages here were deemed to be equal to one to Rome.

The Preseli Hills, a major landscape feature in the National Park.

4. Preseli Hills and the North

Standing on the rocky, burial cairn-topped Foel Cwmcerwyn, at 1758ft/536m the reigning summit of the Preseli Hills, towering above the plantations of the Pantmaenog Forest, you could be a million miles from the sheltered, sandy beaches of the Pembrokeshire Coast.

Naked crags of dolerite, rhyolite and volcanic ashes from the Ordovician period, laid down perhaps 450 million years ago, break through the heather, gorse and bracken in distinctive rocky tors, to make this part of the National Park feel more like Dartmoor than Dyfed.

It was from these strange, other-worldly outcrops on places like Carn Menyn, two miles along the Cerrigmarchogion-Mynydd Bach ridge to the east, that the bluestones in Stonehenge's inner circle were quarried and somehow transported to Wiltshire (see box p33). The blocky nature of the rocks would seem to make them ideally suited to such use, but the site must have been sacred in some way for the prehistoric builders of Wiltshire to have come so far to obtain them.

The Preselis certainly have an atmosphere and feeling unlike anywhere else in the National Park and, some would say, in Britain. Myths and legends haunt the rocky summits like the mists which so often wreathe them. The place names on that main ridge between Foel Cwmcerwyn in the west and hillfort-encircled Foel Drygarn, overlooking Crymych and the infant Taf in the east, are significant.

First you pass Cerrigmarchogion, or 'the rocks of the knights', which is said to mark the place where the mythical boar Twrch Trwyth slew several of King Arthur's knights – and then turned them into stone. One of the many alleged sites of Arthur's grave is the ancient cairn known as Bedd Arthur, on the ridge just beyond Carn Bica, while Carn Arthur stands on the moorland slopes just to the south-east.

Carn Ingli, a rocky outlier which overlooks Newport and its bay and towers over its extensive common, is also known as the Angel's Peak. The low walled enclosures and hut circles may date from the Iron Age. It was here that St Brynach, a fifth-century Irish monk, is said to have communed with angels.

Foel Cwmcerwyn summit – the highest point in Pembrokeshire.

Running west from the Preselis towards Fishguard and the sea is the beautiful wooded valley of the Gwaun (Cwm Gwaun), which was formed as a meltwater channel beneath the glaciers of the last Ice Age perhaps 10,000 years ago. The tiny River Gwaun seems almost too insignificant to have carved out such an impressive valley, but the reason lies in its birth as a raging, icy torrent which created the deep, narrow valley we see today.

In addition to its valuable semi-natural oakwoods, so important for wildlife, the Gwaun Valley is also important for its

A rushing stream in the impressive Gwaun Valley (Cwm Gwaun).

The intricately-carved Celtic cross in Nevern churchyard.

Lower Fishguard, which masqueraded as Dylan Thomas's famous village in Under Milk Wood.

prehistory. At Parc y Meirw ('The field of the dead'), near Llanychaer, an alignment of 'male' and 'female' standing stones would rival Avebury in Wiltshire or Carnac in Brittany if it were bigger and better known.

The Perpendicular parish church at nearby Nevern is dedicated to St Brynach and in the churchyard stands the magnificent 13-feet high Nevern Cross, dating from the tenth century and covered with the most intricate Celtic knotwork carvings. You approach the church through an avenue of dark, gnarled yews, one of which is known as the Bleeding Yew because it drips blood-red sap. Nevern was once the administrative centre of the area; the headquarters of the Welsh Hundred of Cemais and later the Norman lord Robert Fitz-Martin, who built the motte and bailey castle in the early twelfth century.

Downstream from Nevern is Newport (Trefdraeth), on the estuary of the River Nyfer which rises beneath the Preselis. This is an ancient township complete with ruined thirteenth-

Ponies graze the slopes overlooking Dinas Island.

century castle, and it still elects a mayor who, with others, 'beats the bounds' of the parish every May. Newport Sands is a popular beach for bathing, windsurfing and boating.

Prehistoric man certainly seems to have found this area of the National Park to his liking, for between the town of Newport and the river bridge stands the Carreg Coetan Arthur cromlech, while a mile to the west there is a unique circle of five Neolithic cromlechau known as Cerrig y Gof.

Further inland about 4 miles to the south-east of Newport stands one of the most famous of all the Pembrokeshire cromlechs, Pentre Ifan. The megalithic 'coffee table' we see today, with its 16-tonne capstone standing over seven feet high on its massive 'legs', is the skeleton of the monument, which originally would have been covered by an earthen mound. Like other Pembrokeshire cromlechs, Pentre Ifan was the burial place for an important leader in the area perhaps 5000 years ago.

Although the busy Irish ferry harbour of Fishguard (Abergwaun) is excluded from the National Park, many visitors stay there and enjoy the pretty cottages in the Lower Town, which doubled as 'Llaregeb' in the 1971 film of Dylan Thomas's *Under Milk Wood*. The Fishguard area was the scene in 1797 of the last farcical attempted invasion of Britain by a motley army of French troops which landed at Carregwastad Point, and the pub in the town square where the surrender was signed still proudly boasts the fact.

Between Fishguard Bay and Newport Bay, the rocky headland known as Dinas Island (National Trust) is in fact not an island but joined to the mainland by the valley which runs between Cwm-y-Eglwys and Pwllgwaelod. Formerly known as Ynys Fach Llyffan ('the little island of the giant, Llyffan'), Dinas Island was the setting for R.M. Lockley's books *Island Farm* and *The Golden Year*. The walk to the summit of Pen y Fan on the headland of Dinas Head is well worth the effort, as it is the haunt of wheeling buzzards and ravens.

The Stonehenge Bluestones

How the famous inner ring of 80, 5-ton bluestones were transported the 180 miles from their source on the bleak summits of the Preseli Hills to far-off Stonehenge on Salisbury Plain in Wiltshire is a question which still generates argument among archaeologists, geologists and historians. Were they brought down from the Preselis for transportation by sea around St Davids Head and into the Bristol Channel, then up the rivers Avon and Wylye to Stonehenge? Or were they, as some imagine, carried there as natural 'erratics' by Ice Age glaciers? As the last glaciation did not reach Salisbury Plain, the latter explanation now seems unlikely.

The twin hills are prominent features of Ramsey Island, long linked with nearby St Davids.

5. The Islands

Most of the seven main islands off the Pembrokeshire Coast were given their names by Viking or Scandinavian raiders, who probably used them as landmarks as they maraudered along the fringes of the Celtic Sea.

Thus the 'holm' suffix of Skokholm, Grassholm and Gateholm comes from the Danish or Old Scandinavian for 'a small island', while the names of Caldey, Ramsey and Skomer also come from the Norse tongue. The only exception is St Margaret's, the small island off Caldey once known as Little Caldey, where there was a small chapel dedicated to St Margaret first recorded in the fourteenth century.

All but one – Caldey – are now uninhabited except for the seasonal wardens of their bird reserves during the summer months. The western isles of Ramsey, Skomer and Skokholm are all famous for their seabirds, best seen during May, June and July, their colonies of grey seals, and their abundance of wildflowers, which burst into glorious bloom in spring and early summer.

After Gateholm, which can be reached on foot at low tide, Caldey and Skomer are the most accessible of Pembrokeshire's islands, reached by regular boat services during the summer season from Tenby and Martin's Haven, near Marloes, respectively. Trips to the more remote Skokholm and Grassholm bird reserves must be booked in advance.

Close neighbours and bird islands supreme – Skokholm (above) and Skomer.

Caldey Island viewed from Lydstep.

Easily the most popular trip to the Pembrokeshire islands is the short, 2-mile excursion from Tenby to Caldey across Caldey Roads to the south. Caldey has been farmed by the Cistercian monks of the whitewashed and pantiled-roofed abbey since 1929. Before that, the Italianate abbey buildings were a home of the Benedictine order, which had been there since the twelfth century. The tiny Norman Priory Church behind the abbey, with its distinctive leaning spire, dates from this period.

Visitors can chat to the friendly, white-robed monks during their visit, and take advantage of the excellent restaurant and shop, where the unique perfume and delicious chocolate manufactured by the monks on the island can be purchased. After looking around the abbey and shop, it is well worth taking the short walk up the lane to Chapel Point and the white-painted lighthouse.

Surprisingly, Skomer is the biggest Welsh island after Anglesey in the north. Situated off the Dale-Marloes peninsula, it covers 722 acres (292 ha) and since 1959 has been a National Nature Reserve, having been farmed up until 1958. It is reached by a sometimes choppy boat ride from Martin's Haven to the sheltered inlet of North Haven.

Undoubtedly the best time to visit Skomer is in the spring or early summer, when the whole of the interior of the island is blanketed with a carpet of the misty blue of blue-bells and the rich claret of red campions. The grassy paths that lead through the fields of flowers are a springy delight,

External and internal views of the Italianate Caldey Abbey.

A floral sea of bluebells delights Skomer visitors in spring.

Close company – a few of the estimated 30,000 plus pairs of gannets on Grassholm.

and the easy, 3-mile walk around the island is thoroughly recommended.

You will be rewarded with close-up views of puffin, guillemot and razorbill, while the cliffs echo with the high-pitched calls of chough, jackdaw and gulls, in what has been described as one of the finest seabird colonies in north-west Europe. The puffins which zip in and out of the deep defile on the south coast known as The Wick are virtually tame and take little notice of visitors. The rocky islets of the Garland Stone in the north and the Mew Stone in the south are the best places to see cliff-nesting birds and the occasional exciting glimpse of breaching off-shore porpoises.

Usually unseen because of their nocturnal habits is the huge colony of Manx shearwaters, which has been estimated at over 100,000 pairs. Seals are another common sight, especially near the Garland Stone, Pigstone Bay and South Haven, basking on the sun-drenched rocks like overweight holidaymakers.

Skomer is also famous for its rabbits, introduced to Britain by the Normans who constructed special cigar-shaped pillow mounds as artificial burrows. Some of the first permanent settlers on Skomer were the warreners who looked after the rabbits, but hut circles and ancient field systems tell of a much earlier farming community which dates back at least 2000 years ago to the Iron Age. Later human remains include two lime kilns and the old, farmhouse in the centre of the island, which dates to the early eighteenth century.

Another large colony of Manx shearwaters nests on Skokholm, a Wildlife Trust South and West Wales Nature Reserve to the south of Skomer, which is reached by catching a bookable boat from Martin's Haven. Skokholm lays claim to being Britain's first bird observatory, established in 1933 by the writer and naturalist R.M. Lockley, who lived on and farmed the island between 1927 and 1939 (see box below).

The most remote of the Pembrokeshire islands is Grassholm, which lies 7 miles to the west of Skomer and is now owned and managed as a nature reserve by the RSPB. It is most famous for its enormous gannetry, which numbers around 30,000 pairs and covers much of the interior of the rocky island in a squabbling mass of birds. Other breeding birds include kittiwake, razorbill, guillemot, shag and three species of gulls.

Ramsey Island, a constantly visible landmark from the St Davids Peninsula, is quite unlike the flat-topped Skomer and Skokholm, and is dominated by its twin hills of Carn Ysgubor and Carn Llundain. It can be visited by using the summertime boats from Porthstinian, west of St Davids. Its beaches are the favoured breeding grounds for the colony of grey seals in the autumn.

The last of the major Pembrokeshire islands is Gateholm, which is accessible on foot from the western end of Marloes Sands near Gateholm Stack at low tide. There are barely visible remains of an ancient Celtic monastic settlement on the island, and it offers a fine view east to the Dale peninsula down to St Ann's Head and north to Skomer and Midland Isle.

Dream Island Days

Pembrokeshire naturalist and author, R.M. (Ronald) Lockley moved with his wife to Skokholm in 1927, and six years later set up the first bird observatory in Britain there. The couple spent an idyllic twelve years recording birds and farming on the island, and writing about their experiences in *Dream Island* and *Island Days*, published in 1930 and 1934 respectively. These were followed by a series of further evocative books.

The late Ronald Lockley on a return visit to Skokholm in the 1980s.

Thrift provides just one of the many pastel shades on the Pembrokeshire Coast.

6. Wildlife of Pembrokeshire

It was the celebrated Pembrokeshire naturalist and author, R.M. Lockley, who described the dream of living 'alone with birds and flowers in some remote place where they were plentiful and undisturbed.' It was a dream he was to realise when he moved with his wife Doris to the Pembrokeshire island of Skokholm in 1927, and later set up the first bird observatory in Britain there.

There could be no better place for the Pembrokeshire Coast and particularly its string of rocky islands is richly endowed with both bird and floral life. There are internationally important colonies of gannets, Manx shearwaters, storm petrel, chough and peregrine falcon which are attracted by the safe, rocky cliff-sites for nesting and the abundant supplies of marine plankton which sustain the fish on which the birds feed – and indirectly their predators like the dashing peregrine.

The world's largest breeding population of the now internationally-rare Manx shearwater are found on Skomer, Skokholm and Middleholm. These strange nocturnal underground nesters often utilise old rabbit burrows for their homes, and their odd, other-worldly cries as they return to their burrows gave them the local names of cuckee or cuckles.

Other underground nesters are the comical puffin – looking like a cross between a miniature penguin and a parrot – which nest in great numbers on Skomer and the other islands. Their favourite food is sand eels, but how they manage to line them

A comical puffin returns with another beak-full of sand eels.

The lifeboat house and slipway at St Justinian, located on the Coast Path.

up so neatly in their bright, black, red and yellow striped bill after hunting trips is still a mystery. The comparative absence of puffins and shearwaters from the mainland and Ramsey and Caldey is because their burrow-nesting habits would make them easy prey for the endemic rats, foxes and stoats.

Grassholm, the most remote, craggy and inhospitable of the islands 7 miles off the Marloes peninsula, often looks as if it is capped by snow, however unlikely that might seem in the mild Atlantic climate. On other occasions, it seems to have a white halo of cloud stationed above it, but neither of these apparent phenomena is true.

The fact is that Grassholm is home to one of the largest colonies of gannets in the world, and the 'snow' staining the top of the island is nothing more than their guano. And that white cloud is when the estimated 33,000 breeding pairs take to the air above the island. Watching these elegant, goose-sized birds feeding is one of the most spectacular sights in nature, as they plummet in a vertical, 100-foot power-dive into the shoals of fish, folding their six-foot wings back into a lethal arrow at the very moment of impact.

The mysterious storm petrel used to be known by sailors as Mother Carey's chicken, after a fabled witch of the high seas, and this insignificant little bird was a particular favourite of Lockley. 'I have a great affection for this little bird which is no bigger than a sparrow and yet can ride out the endless hurricanes of the Atlantic winter,' he wrote. There were about 1000 breeding pairs of storm petrels on Skokholm in Lockley's day, and they spend most of their days out at sea feeding close to the surface, apparently 'walking' on the water like little St Peters – hence their name.

Birds found on the rocky island and coastal cliffs include that most elegant member of the crow family, the scarlet-billed and legged chough, a master of the swirling air currents which constantly sweep up against the cliffs, and its menacing, croaking cousin, the raven.

Much more common are the similar looking cormorants and shags, while some of the tiniest and most improbable ledges are occupied by razorbills, another penguin-like large, black and white member of the auk family which provides the National Park Authority with its logo – affectionately known as 'Reggie.'

They can be seen most commonly on the Elegug Stacks near the Green Bridge of Wales on the Castlemartin peninsula, where they share their precarious home with colonies of guille-

Coastal sightings: porpoise in Ramsey Sound (above) and common dolphin (below). The illustration (above left) is a sunfish.

Foxglove and gorse.

mots, fulmars, shags and kittiwakes, whose onomatopoeic cries echo around the cliffs.

Grey seals are the largest and most interesting mammals you are likely to see in the National Park, and Ramsey Island boasts the second-largest colony in southern Britain. It's not uncommon to see the bobbing head of a seal watching you as you walk along the Coast Path, and the sight of the pure white pups on Ramsey, Skomer or in secluded bays is guaranteed to attract the 'ahh' factor.

Out at sea, the common porpoise is often seen, and less commonly, dolphins. The impressive sight of a basking shark – one of the world's largest fish – can be the reward of a boat trip to the islands in summer. More recently, sightings have increased of the strange, disc-like sunfish – usually about the size of a dustbin lid – which spends most of its life feeding on jellyfish in the deep oceans.

The largest land mammals are fox and badger, and otters breed along the quiet river valleys of the Gwaun and Nevern.

Lockley's requirement for flowers along with his birds is met in the most spectacular fashion in the Pembrokeshire Coast National Park. You will find flowering plants in bloom in any month of the year here, from the ubiquitous golden yellow of the gorse, with that wonderful pineapple smell, to the swathes of red and white campion and misty bluebells which carpet the rolling slopes of Skomer and the coastal clifftops in spring and early summer.

A patchwork of colours, from the delicate pink of the thrift and sea pinks to the subtle yellow of primroses, and from the orange-red bird's foot trefoil to the bright white oxeye daisies,

Coastline daisies.

One of many waterlilies in Bosherston Ponds.

paint the clifftops in a floral display unmatched by anywhere in the British Isles.

With the wealth of wild flowers come beautiful butterflies, such as peacock, red admiral and tortoiseshell, along with the rarer dark green fritillaries, skippers and common blues.

And the famous lily ponds at Bosherston are the haunt of many beautifully-iridescent dragonflies and damselflies, which hover above the white lily flowers like miniature prehistoric helicopters.

Celtic Creatures

Look more closely at that smooth grey boulder lying on a rocky Pembrokeshire beach and you may see it move. For that 'boulder' can often turn out to be a grey seal, as Pembrokeshire is the home to one of the largest breeding colonies in Britain. The first white-furred, liquid-eyed pups are born in August at the height of the tourist season, and as pupping continues into September, the barking of adult females will often be heard along the coast. One of the biggest breeding colonies is on Ramsey Island, but they can also be seen at Deer Park near Marloes and elsewhere. Tagging has shown that pups may swim as far away as Ireland, Brittany or Spain within a few months of their birth – truly Celtic creatures.

Seal pup.

Reconstructed roundhouses at Castell Henllys Iron Age Fort.

7. A Pembrokeshire Timeline

10,000–8000 YEARS AGO
PALAEOLITHIC (OLD STONE) AGE

The first hunter-gatherers move into Pembrokeshire following the retreat of the Ice Age glaciers. Earliest evidence of them is found in caves such as Cat's Hole at Monkton, Hoyle's Mouth near Tenby and on Caldey Island. Finds have included primitive stone tools and butchered animal bones.

8000–5000 YEARS AGO
MESOLITHIC (MIDDLE STONE) AGE

Tiny scatters of flint known as microliths are recorded near Solva, on Nab Head near St Brides, and on the banks of the River Nyfer at Newport, providing the only evidence of the Mesolithic hunter-gatherers who hunted along the coast for game.

5000–4000 YEARS AGO
NEOLITHIC (NEW STONE) AGE

The first true farmers arrive, probably in skin-covered boats like modern coracles, and live in small communities such as that discovered at Clegyr Boia, near St Davids. The most impressive remains of their passing are the large burial monuments known as cromlechs, such as Pentre Ifan on the northern slopes of the Preselis and Carreg Samson, near Abercastle.

4000–3000 YEARS AGO
BRONZE AGE

There are many Bronze Age burial mounds or tumuli in Pembrokeshire, often on hilltops or ridges, most notably at Foel Drygarn in the Preseli Hills, and on the ridgeway between Tenby and Pembroke. They contained the distinctive cremation pottery typical of the period.

3000–2000 YEARS AGO
IRON AGE

The age of the hillforts, with fine examples around the Preselis at rocky Carn Ingli above Newport, on the summit of Foel Drygarn, and at the site brilliantly reconstructed by the National Park at Castell Henllys. At Carn Llidi, near St Davids, walls built during the Iron Age are still in use, and there are similar 2000-year-old field systems on Skomer.

2000 YEARS AGO
ROMANS

Carmarthen is the site of the most westerly Roman fort so far discovered in South Wales, and a single Romano British farmstead has been excavated at Trelessy, above Amroth.

2000–1000 YEARS AGO
DARK AGES

The falsely-named Dark Ages saw the flowering of Christianity in Pembrokeshire, led by St David or *Dewi Sant*, who was born around AD500, and moved his monastery from Whitesand Bay to Glyn Rhosyn, the site of St David's Cathedral, where he was buried after his death in 588. Carved crosses such as at Carew and Nevern are set up, Runic inscriptions appear, and Norse raiders gave their names to Skokholm, Grassholm and Dale.

Top left: *Pentre Ifan, in winter's grip.*

Top right: *Visitors discover what it was like to live in the Iron Age at Castell Henllys.*

Below left: *Carreg Samson, near Mathry.*

Below right: *Coetan Arthur, Manorbier.*

1000–1200AD
NORMANS

The Norman conquerors build the first motte and bailey and shell keep castles, as at Wiston, followed by more substantial structures such as those at Pembroke, Cilgerran, Haverfordwest, Tenby and Manorbier. The 'Landsker' separates the 'Englishry' in the south from the 'Welshry' in the north, and the first manor houses and churches are built.

1200–1400
MIDDLE AGES

Markets are set up in the major villages, such as Pembroke and Haverfordwest, and farming and fishing become the mainstay of the local economy. Other local industries include lime burning, and woollen and corn mills.

1400–1700
TUDORS AND STUARTS

The age of the large landowners and the creation of country houses, as medieval castles like Carew are 'domesticated' by the insertion of mullioned windows, with the need for defence becoming less important. From Tudor times, coastal villages become involved in trading around the Bristol Channel and across the Irish Sea. Silver and lead are mined near St Davids, and the first slate quarries appear.

1700–1850
INDUSTRIAL REVOLUTION

The last invasion of Britain takes place near Fishguard in 1797. Coal becomes the 'black gold' of the Industrial Revolution, and pits which had been worked on a small scale since medieval times are expanded as industrialists seek out the high quality anthracite found near the coast, which is easily transported via the Bristol Channel, from ports like Nolton Haven. Iron ore is also extracted between Saundersfoot and Amroth, and slate from ports such as Abereiddi and Abercastle.

The splendid eleventh-century Celtic cross at Carew.

VICTORIAN BRITAIN

Further expansion of the coal industry. The first major disaster occurs at the Garden Pit, Landshipping, when the River Cleddau bursts into the workings killing 40 men. Pembroke Dock becomes the Royal Dockyard and Milford Haven develops as a major waterway and fishing port. The Railway Age dawns, and Brunel pushes the Great Western Railway through to Fishguard, Pembroke and Milford Haven, bringing the first tourists.

1900–TO DATE
MODERN BRITAIN

The military takes over the Castlemartin Ranges for training, flying boats are based at Pembroke Dock and during the Second World War airfields are built on coastal locations. The fast-expanding populations of South Wales use their increased leisure time to visit the coastal resorts in ever greater numbers. The Pembrokeshire Coast National Park – the fifth in Britain – is designated in 1952, and the Pembrokeshire Coast Path opens in 1970.

Porthgain's harbour and ruined brickworks are industrial gems.

The 'Blue Lagoon' at Abereiddi is actually a drowned quarry.

Manorbier – one of the finest in a 'county of castles'.

Pembroke Castle – birthplace of Henry Tudor, who became King Henry VII.

The Castles of Pembrokeshire

One of the most interesting aspects of Pembrokeshire for visitors is the wonderful collection of medieval castles which dominate the landscape. They range from the early shell keep on its wooded motte at Wiston, to the very substantial structures of Pembroke, Carew, Manorbier and Haverfordwest. Most were 'slighted' during the Civil War, but still retain their air of domination over the landscape.

The first castles were built by the Normans but over the years they were enlarged and refortified into the later medieval curtain walled structures such as Pembroke, Haverfordwest and Manorbier. Later still, windows were added as they were converted to country houses, such as at Carew. Most of Pembrokeshire's magnificent castles are open to the public, and are either in the hands of Cadw: Welsh Historic Monuments or private owners (see Where to Go section).

The memorial stone at Carregwastad Point which recalls the 'Last Invasion' by the French in 1797.

8. Myths, Legends and Customs

Perhaps the most persistent and lasting legends of the Pembrokeshire Coast concern St David – or *Dewi Sant* – the patron saint of Wales, who was born to St Non on the south coast of the peninsula which now takes his name.

A fearful storm with lightning, thunder, floods and hail presaged the birth as St Non, a niece of King Arthur, went into labour. But as she gave birth to David, an unearthly light as bright as the sun illuminated the scene and all became calm and still. A spring of crystal-clear water instantly burst forth on the spot.

You can still see that spring high on the clifftop above St Non's Bay to the south of St Davids, where a simple stone arch covers St Non's Well, near the ruins of the medieval chapel in the fields, close to the 1930s' Chapel of Our Lady and St Non. It is still a place of pilgrimage and before the Reformation water from the well was taken and used as holy water at St David's Cathedral.

David was baptised by his cousin, St Elvis, the Bishop of Munster, and educated in the ways of the Church at various ecclesiastical sites in Wales. Almost the only thing known about him was that he was an ascetic, and drank only water and ate mainly bread and herbs. He is said to have stood six feet tall and was strong enough to pull a plough as well as any team of oxen.

As more and more miracles were ascribed to him, the cult of St David spread as far north as Derbyshire and Leominster in England, but it was concentrated in South Wales, Cornwall and Somerset. He returned to Pembrokeshire to build his first church at Tywyn Common on the slopes of Carn Llidi, but after the foundations were destroyed overnight, an angel is said to have advised him to build it at Glyn Rhosyn in the valley of the River Alun, where today's medieval cathedral stands.

Along with his fellow Welsh saints, Padarn and Teilo, he is said to have made a pilgrimage in Jerusalem and other holy shrines, including Rome, and at the synod of Brefi in around 545, he was made chief bishop of Wales. On his way to Brefi, in Cardiganshire, David performed one of his most acclaimed miracles when he restored to life the dead child of a widow.

St Non's Well – still a place of pilgrimage.

That Spartan diet was obviously good for him, for St David is alleged to have lived for 147 years. He died in 588 and was buried in his cathedral church in the west wall of the chapel of the Holy Trinity. After his death, St David became so important as a figure of veneration in the Middle Ages that two pilgrimages here were deemed to be equal to one to Rome.

The connection of David's mother, St Non, with King Arthur echoes another common theme in the folklore of Pembrokeshire. One of the many alleged sites of Arthur's grave is at Bedd Arthur, high on the Preseli ridge, where the rocky outcrop of Cerrigmarchogion, meaning 'the rocks of the knights', is also said to mark the spot where the mythical boar Twrch Trwyth slew several of Arthur's knights and turned them to stone.

The mysterious figure of St Govan, whose tiny thirteenth-century chapel is tucked away under the cliffs west of St Govan's Head, also has Arthurian connections. Some scholars have identified him as the chivalrous Sir Gawaine of the Green Knight story, and the chapel with the 'green chapel' which is the denouement of the story.

Whatever the truth, if you descend the steep, allegedly-uncountable, steps through the cliffs to visit Govan's chapel, you will see the cleft in the rocks into which the shy hermit was said to have disappeared when visitors called, and the well which is supposed to have curative properties. The bell cote once held a silver bell stolen by pirates, which was rescued by sea nymphs and now also lies entombed, like St Govan, in the rocks.

Those sea nymphs – also known as Tylwyth Teg or the Fair Folk – are supposed to inhabit mythical invisible islands out at sea, only coming to the mainland to market their fairy produce at local markets.

Tucked away beneath the cliffs: St Govan's Chapel.

Styles and sizes of Pembrokeshire churches. Top: *Night-time view of St Mary's, Tenby – the largest parish church in Wales.* Left: *Nolton Chapel, close to the shore.* Right: *Pontfaen, a pretty, bell-coted church in the Gwaun Valley.*

Aerial view of Strumble Head with its lighthouse.

Another, this time historical, landfall which has entered the realms of Pembrokeshire folklore is the last invasion of Britain by a foreign power in 1797. The farcical 'landing of the French' at Carregwastad Point near Fishguard was a diversion timed with a rebellion in Ireland – but it all went disastrously wrong. The motley army of about 1400 French convicts commanded by an Irish-American William Tate, looted local farms and got drunk. They were quickly contained by the militia aided by the local population led by the redoubtable Jemima Nicholas, who is said to have captured 14 French soldiers on her own. She is buried in St Mary's churchyard, Fishguard.

The Landsker

An invisible line stretching from Brandy Brook near Newgale in the west to Amroth in the east creates the ancient division in the Pembrokeshire landscape known by the Norse word of 'Landsker'. The land north of the line is sometimes known as 'the Welshry', and the buildings, language and place names are still very Welsh, and even surnames are predominately Welsh. Coastal headlands are known as pens and estuaries have the Welsh prefix aber. To the south of the Landsker, in the area once known as 'the Englishry', settlements and names are generally English-sounding; the churches have English-like four-square towers; the bays are 'havens' and headlands, 'points'. At one time, to marry across the Landsker was strictly frowned upon and something which seldom occurred.

The French surrended after two days at Goodwick Sands and the Pembrokeshire Yeomanry still wears the battle honour of Fishguard – the only British regiment to carry an honour won on British soil.

Forty-five years before the French invasion, Britain adopted the Gregorian calendar but in the beautiful Gwaun Valley local folk still abide by the previous Julian calendar, and celebrate New Year's Day on 13 January – or *Hen Galan.*

And if you are in Pembrokeshire on St David's Day – 1 March – you are likely to see people wearing a daffodil in their lapel and local schoolchildren in national dress, in proud celebration of their locally-born patron saint. There is actually a Tenby daffodil.

The Tenby daffodil.

The unique atmosphere created by a farmers' market.

9. Pembrokeshire Products

There's no better way to experience a true taste of Pembrokeshire than to actually try the produce which comes from the area.

And the best way to do that is to look out for the Pembrokeshire Produce Mark, whose green Celtic cross ribbon logo marks genuine locally-grown or produced products. The Produce Mark provides an instantly recognisable guarantee that what you are tasting is produced locally, so look out for the green circle.

The mark also applies to restaurants and hotels which use local produce in their menus, and to shops and other retail outlets which sell local produce. All these premises are verified to measure their eligibility before they are permitted to display the prized logo.

Those products include top quality beef and lamb, delicious farmhouse cheeses and other dairy products, Pembrokeshire's famous early new potatoes and other vegetables, home-made preserves and even locally-produced wines, all coming from Pembrokeshire's vigorous farming and market gardening community.

The National Park Authority believes that it has an important role to play in promoting high-quality locally-grown food and products, and the environmentally-friendly goods which are produced and processed locally. It believes that this helps to sustain the special landscape quality of the area, while ensuring that the money spent on goods stays within the local economy, so placing an economic value on its landscape management.

As the farming community diversifies more into marketing its own produce, lively farmers' markets have been set up on the Riverside Quay at Haverfordwest on alternate Fridays and at Fishguard Town Hall on alternate Saturdays. This is a great way to meet up with the producers themselves, and to ensure that what you are buying is as fresh and good as you can get.

The markets themselves have a unique atmosphere, taking you back to the time when shopping was fun – and important social events where country people could meet up and share the latest news, as well as sell their produce. Organisers claim that everything on sale has either been grown, reared, caught, brewed, pickled, baked, smoked or processed by stallholders. You can't get much fresher than that!

You can see the cheesemaking process taking place at special demonstrations staged at several local cheesemakers. And the Pembrokeshire County Show, featuring around 4000 animals and over 600 trade stands and exhibits, takes place every August on the County Showground just outside Haverfordwest.

Tasty jams, preserves and cakes are on sale at the Women's Institute markets, which are held during the holiday season at St Davids Memorial Hall on Thursdays; Theatr Gwaun at Fishguard on Tuesdays; Riverside Quay at Haverfordwest on Fridays; the Queen's Hall at Narberth on Thursdays; Pembroke Town Hall on Thursdays; the Pater Hall at Pembroke Dock on Fridays; at Manorbier Village Hall on Wednesdays; The Captains Table at Saundersfoot on Thursdays, and at St John's Church, Tenby, on Fridays.

And as nowhere in Pembrokeshire is more than 10 miles from the sea, you would expect a lively fresh seafood menu – and you will not be disappointed. From scallops to sea bass and from crabs to lobsters, the harvest from Pembrokeshire's bountiful seas is probably unrivalled in Britain.

A special Pembrokeshire Fish Week, an annual celebration of the bounty from the county's sea and rivers, is organised by Pembrokeshire County Council every summer. With events throughout the area, Fish Week caters for everyone who enjoys fish and seafood – from those who catch the fish and those who eat it. Organisers claim that there is something for everyone – for the whole family, the sportsman and the connoisseur – with events ranging from eating the seafood itself, to stories and sea shanties from those who go out on the sea to catch it.

Axeman in action at the County Show.

Fish Week fare.

The area is blessed with a wonderful array of restaurants making eating out one of the great pleasures of a holiday in Pembrokeshire. As you might expect, seafood and seafood restaurants figure strongly in the lists, but there is literally something for everyone in the range and choice of eating houses available.

The beautiful scenery of the Pembrokeshire Coast has inspired artists and craftspeople for centuries, and today, the National

Park is the home of a vigorous creative community. They draw their inspiration from the natural beauty of the area, expressing it in various media ranging from oil and watercolour paintings; wood and stone sculpture; hand-thrown pottery; to hand-made candles or woollen rugs.

The number of artists' galleries in the Pembrokeshire Coast National Park is probably only rivalled in Britain by those in Cornwall across the Bristol Channel. Without exception, they always welcome visitors to admire their personal, and often quite stunning, views of the landscape.

Pembrokeshire Art Associates organises regular travelling exhibitions throughout the area during the year, representing the work of up to 60 locally-based artists. Arts festivals take place in September at Tenby and Pembroke, and in May and June at St Davids, while Fishguard has an international music festival in July.

Folk music is alive and well in Pembrokeshire, linking in to the Celtic peninsula cultures of Brittany, Cornwall, Ireland and Scotland. The Royal Oak in Fishguard is the headquarters of Fishguard Folk, which hosts a folk music festival in May, and Folk at the Fish is a regular event at the Fishguard Arms, Haverfordwest.

The many craftspeople of the area are represented by the Pembrokeshire Craftsmen's Circle or the Pembrokeshire Craft Makers, based at the Waterfront Gallery in Milford Haven Docks. Both these organisations work to protect the growing reputation of their members' work in both quality and innovation.

On a larger scale, the woollen mills at Solva and Tregwynt, Castlemorris, and the Y Felin flour mill at St Dogmaels, welcome visitors to show them their products in the making.

Coracles

The national centre for the building of the circular, skin-covered fishing boats known as coracles is at Cenarth on the River Teifi, south-east of Cardigan to the north of the National Park. These strange little one-man craft are of a very primitive and ancient design, with a wooden framework over which is stretched tarred waterproofed canvas – originally animal skins. It takes many years of experience to learn how to propel them in a straight line, using the single wooden paddle both for steering and propulsion. Cilgerran, set in its beautiful wooded gorge just downstream from Cenarth, is still the venue of an annual coracle 'regatta', where local fishermen compete in races on the Teifi.

Skilled hands are needed to propel a coracle.

St Brides Bay panorama.

10. Leave the Car Behind

Traffic congestion may be a severe problem in most National Parks, though in the Pembrokeshire Coast it is generally a very localised issue in the peak holiday time.

But if you want to be a truly 'green' visitor and wherever possible leave your car behind, the Pembrokeshire Coastal Bus Services and the Park's park-and-ride services to Tenby and St Davids can really open up the National Park for you, avoiding the stress of queuing and finding somewhere to park.

Running seven days a week throughout the main holiday season, the Coastal Bus Services were introduced by Pembrokeshire Greenways, a partnership which includes Pembrokeshire County Council, the Pembrokeshire Coast National Park Authority, the Countryside Council for Wales, the National Trust, and PLANED. Services have been extended recently to run for three days a week throughout the winter and spring.

Roadside congestion, Freshwater West.

The buses, which include the Strumble Shuttle, the Poppit Rocket, the Puffin Shuttle and the Coastal Cruiser, are designed to encourage both local people and visitors to enjoy car-free travel along the length of the coast. And it is an ideal way to explore sections of the famous linear Coast Path, without ever having to retrace your steps.

In 2005/06 nearly 59,000 people used the Coastal Bus Services – which meant that there were up to 25,000 fewer cars clogging up the Park's often narrow roads. All the coastal buses welcome dog passengers (at the driver's discretion), so Fido can come along too, and the competitive prices include day-rover tickets for multiple journeys.

Best of all, the reaction of both the public and local people to the new bus services has been universally enthusiastic. The bus drivers receive high praise in surveys for the information they provide 'on wheels'.

The Strumble Shuttle service (No. 404) between Fishguard and St Davids, calls at Strumble Head, Tregwynt Woollen Mill, Abercastle, Porthgain, Llanrhian, Abereiddi beach and St

Coastal buses provide a very popular and growing service.

Davids, and back in the opposite direction. The Poppit Rocket (Service 405) runs between Cardigan and St Dogmaels, Poppit Sands, Newport, Dinas Cross and Fishguard.

The Puffin Shuttle (No. 400), which gives the service its logo of a boot-clad puffin striding out along the path, runs daily between St Davids and Milford Haven, calling at Solva, Newgale, Druidston Haven, Broad Haven, Little Haven, St Brides, Dale, Marloes and St Ishmaels. The Coastal Cruiser (Service 387) links Pembroke with Angle, Bosherston, Stackpole, Freshwater and back again to Pembroke. The so-called 'surf bus' has an internal rack to carry surf boards, and it can also accommodate two bicycles and is wheelchair-accessible.

The Celtic Coaster is another wheelchair-accessible minibus which runs around the St Davids Peninsula, calling at St Davids, Porth Clais, St Justinians and Whitesands, enabling you to catch the boat trips to Ramsey Island.

Other bus services in the south of Pembrokeshire include the 356 Milford Haven to Pembroke route; the 349/359 Haverfordwest – Pembroke – Tenby service; the 350 Tenby –

Even surfers use the bus.

Saundersfoot – Amroth service, and the 351 Tenby – Saundersfoot – Amroth – Pendine service.

Train services link Narberth with Tenby, Pembroke, Pembroke Dock, Milford Haven, Haverfordwest and Fishguard. More details of all public transport services, including rail links, can be obtained from any Tourist Information Centre or from the Greenways Office, on 01437 776313. A useful website www.pembrokeshiregreenways.co.uk, gives more up-to-date information on public transport.

The introduction of the free park-and-ride services at St Davids and Tenby has made a big difference to traffic congestion in these two most popular towns in the National Park. During a record year in 2005, almost 100,000 passengers were carried by the two services – 67,000 of them in Tenby.

That meant that about 17,000 cars were taken off Tenby's narrow streets thanks to the park-and-ride service, and congestion was also considerably eased in St Davids – Britain's smallest city.

The Tenby service operates between the Salterns car park (charge) and South Parade, every quarter of an hour between 10am and 6pm in the main season. Pembrokeshire County Council also runs a park-and-ride service at Tenby between the Butts Field car park and the Harbour, during the time that the ancient walled town is pedestrianised.

A Coast Path sign.

The St Davids service runs between The Grove (charge) and Merryvale car parks, every quarter of an hour between 10am and 4pm in the main season. Access to the cathedral from Merrivale is suitable for the less mobile as well as wheelchair users, avoiding steep inclines.

Walkers join the Puffin Shuttle.

A school group takes to the Coast Path on the Pencaer Peninsula.

11. What to Do

As already stated, the best way to appreciate the wonders of the Pembrokeshire Coast National Park is to walk all, or at least part of, the 186-mile Pembrokeshire Coast Path National Trail (see box p71), which is described below.

The trail is often walked from north to south, and the first day between St Dogmaels and Newport is one of the most strenuous. Covering over 15 miles, you negotiate more than 3000 feet (915m) over some of the highest cliffs in Pembrokeshire, including Cemaes Head, Pen yr Afr and Foel Goch. At the end of this long day, you drop down to the broad Newport Sands (Treath Mawr) and over the Iron Bridge into Parrog, the 'old' port of Newport, on the estuary of the Afon Nyfer.

Day two of the path takes the walker west towards Dinas Head, where there is an optional excursion to the 466ft/142m summit of Pen y Fan on the tip of the peninsula, with its fantastic views and possible sightings of seals, porpoises and dolphins in the sea below. Westwards again, you approach the sheltered harbour of Fishguard, with its three areas of Cwm, Penyraber and Abergwaun/Fishguard itself.

Another long day (over 17 miles) faces the walker between Fishguard and Trefin, first north toward Pen Anglas and then west passing Carregwastad Point, the scene of the last unsuccessful invasion of Britain in 1797, and the gloriously wild section of the coast around Strumble Head with its white-painted lighthouse and the lovely bay of Pwll Deri. Heading south now,

Coasteering near Caerfai, St Davids.

A guided walk on the spectacular Castlemartin Army Range.

the path climbs over the headland of Penbwchdy before dropping down to the sandy beach of Aber Mawr and around Mynydd Morfa to Abercastle with the impressive Neolithic cromlech of Carreg Samson just inland.

From Trefin, the path heads west again towards Whitesands Bay, passing Porthgain's impressive industrial relics, the Abereiddi slate quarries, and the Caerau and Castell Coch hill-forts. You now approach the windswept peninsula of St Davids Head, passing the Neolithic burial chamber of Coetan Arthur and the prominent inland hill of Carn Llidi before dropping down to one of Pembrokeshire's finest sandy beaches at Whitesands Bay.

The next section heads south from Whitesands Bay down Ramsey Sound, with fine views of the island to the west, passing the treacherous straits and rip tide known as The Bitches, and then east, passing Porth Clais and St Non's Bay, the birthplace of St David, along the coast to the delightful 'ria' or drowned estuary of Solva.

The 12 miles between Solva and Little Haven takes in the spectacular Iron Age promontory fort of Dinas Fawr, over the 2-mile long Newgale Beach, and then south to the former coal-exporting port of Nolton Haven. Then it's south again past more spectacular coastal scenery until you reach the popular bathing beach of Broad Haven, with Little Haven just beyond it.

The path now turns west to Borough Head, descending to St Brides Haven and across the neck of The Nab and then down to the glorious expanse of sandy beach of Musselwick Bay. West again to Martin's Haven, the departure point for boat trips to Skomer, to the east of the walled former Deer Park of the St Brides Estate. Now we head south passing Gateholm Island to the extensive Marloes Sands beach, with its famous geological feature of the Three Chimneys, and south again to skirt around the Dale peninsula and St Ann's Head.

From Dale the path goes round the Pickleridge lagoons and then east passing the ancient hamlet of St Ishmaels and Great and Little Castle Heads on the coast to cut inland again around the Sandy Haven estuary via Herbrandston. You now have to skirt the huge Milford Haven oil refinery inland from Gelliswick and soon you are passing through Milford Haven town, leaving via Black Bridge. Passing close to one of the new LNG facilities, the path follows the road into Neyland, before crossing the Westfield Pill bridge and then the imposing Cleddau Bridge which spans the main river.

The route now follows a town trail through Pembroke Dock before heading towards castle-crowned Pembroke, then west to reach open country again at Quiots Mill and on past the giant Texaco refinery to Angle Bay beyond Pwllcrochan. After Angle, the path goes around the peninsula passing East Block House and Sheep Island to approach the Castlemartin Training Ranges, where it turns inland to Castlemartin. You must check for firing schedules if you wish to turn south to visit the Green Bridge of Wales, the Elegug Stacks and St Govan's Chapel.

Sea canoeing.

Windsurfing off Tenby.

Bosherston's beautiful lily ponds, created by the Earl of Cawdor in the eighteenth century, are next on the path as it heads east to Stackpole Head and on to Freshwater East Bay, Manorbier, Lydstep Point, South Beach and eventually into Tenby. It is now only just over 7 miles to the trail end at Amroth, via Saundersfoot and Coppet Hall.

The National Park Authority publishes ten pocket-sized guides to sections of the Coast Path and a handy mileage chart, in addition to other walks leaflets. Of course, there are many other fine walks in the National Park, and the Authority also runs an extensive activities and events programme throughout the year (details in the free newspaper *Coast to Coast*). And the National Park's excellent website (www.pembrokeshirecoast.org.uk) describes well over 100 walks with maps, covering over 350 miles of walking routes in all. The maps can be downloaded on your computer at home.

For disabled people and those who find access difficult, a special booklet entitled *Easy Access Routes* is available from information centres. It also includes viewpoints which have easy access.

The main areas for rock climbing in the Park are on the limestone sea cliffs around Castlemartin and on the gabbro and dolerite of the north coast, especially around St Brides Bay and St Davids and Strumble Heads.

If pedal power is your thing, then Pembrokeshire has much to offer. Weatherproof maps to routes between 15 and 35 miles

Cliff climbing on the Castlemartin range.

are available, and there are cycle hire centres, including mountain bikes, at various locations including Newport, Haverfordwest and Kilgetty. The western end of the Celtic Trail is at Fishguard and a continuous cycle route goes through South Wales for 214 miles to Chepstow on the English border.

Many people prefer real horse power, and a variety of stables provide horses, equipment and training to enjoy the National Park from horseback. A network of ancient bridleways gives access to some of the finest countryside, whether you are just pony trekking or a more experienced rider.

You would expect that a mainly coastal Park like Pembrokeshire would be well provided for water sports – and you would not be wrong. Surfers love the broad bays and crashing breakers of beaches like Freshwater West, Broad Haven, Manorbier and Tenby South, while wave-jumping windsurfers are often found enjoying the same beaches.

Sailing, canoeing and kayaking are becoming increasingly popular around the sheltered – and not so sheltered – havens and bays of the Pembrokeshire Coast, and there is a thriving boating industry to supply would-be boaters. Finally, the new adrenalin sport of coasteering has recently become popular in Pembrokeshire. It involves traversing sea cliffs at just above sea level, and combines climbing with scrambling, sea bathing and, if all else fails, cliff-jumping into the sea!

The Pembrokeshire Coast Path

The Pembrokeshire Coast Path was officially opened by the broadcaster and author Wynford Vaughan Thomas, on 16 May, 1970, and followed seventeen years of negotiations and preparations on the 186-mile route. When the National Park Authority was designated in 1952, the task of surveying the proposed path to follow the coast as closely as possible was entrusted to the respected local author and naturalist Ronald Lockley, and his report was enthusiastically accepted by the Countryside Commission in the summer of Coronation Year, 1953. More than 100 footbridges needed to be built, 479 stiles were installed and many thousands of steps were cut into the steeper slopes.

Visitors enjoying an Iron Age experience at Castell Henllys.

12. Where to Go

Although most of the attractions of the Pembrokeshire Coast National Park are quite properly out of doors, recent years have seen a boom in tourist attractions in and around the Park, giving many 'rainy day alternatives' for visitors.

The National Park Authority has led the way in the sensitive provision of these, notably at the award-winning **Castell Henllys Iron Age Fort**, situated on a beautiful wooded spur overlooking Nant Duad at Eglwyswrw, near Newport, where archaeological digs have taken place every summer for over twenty years. Today, lively and accurate reconstructions take place daily in the village of thatched roundhouses, showing visitors what life was really like in Pembrokeshire over 2000 years ago.

Special children's activities are also regularly staged, enabling younger visitors to undertake tasks and games which reflect what might have taken place during the Iron Age, while local crafts-people recreate traditional skills such as spinning and weaving.

Other prehistoric sites in the Park worth visiting include the Neolithic tombs at **Carreg Samson,** near Longhouse Farm, Mathry (SM 848335); **Pentre Ifan,** near Nevern (SN 099370); **Carn Llidi,** near St Davids Head (SM 736279) and **Carreg Coetan Arthur** (Arthur's Quoit) near Pen-y-Bont, Newport (SN 061394).

Another historic site in the management of the National Park Authority and with a lively range of interpretive events during the summer season is **Carew Castle,** romantically sited on the tidal reaches of the Carew River east of Pembroke.

This ruinous but still stately castle, originally dating from the twelfth century but successively 'modernised' through to the late-sixteenth century when the mullioned windows were added, is leased to the National Park Authority by the Carew Estate. A full programme of tours, fairs, events and activities is staged throughout the holiday season, and has included an audience with Sir John Perrot – a favourite at the court of Elizabeth I before ending up in disgrace in the Tower of London – who was responsible for the last 'modernisation' of Carew in Tudor times.

Nearby is the **Carew Tidal Mill**, also managed by the National Park Authority, and within the castle grounds is the ancient **Carew Cross**, one of the finest Celtic crosses in Wales and dedicated to King Maredudd, son of Edwin, a much earlier lord of the manor of Carew.

Like other parts of Wales, Pembrokeshire needed to be subdued by the Norman overlords after the Conquest, and therefore it is not surprising that it has a superb collection of castles.

Senior among these is **Pembroke Castle**, originally built by Gerald de Windsor in the early-twelfth century, and the home of the earls of Pembroke since 1138. Pembroke, complete with curtain walls, barbican and circular Great Keep, had been the chief stronghold of Parliamentary forces during the Civil War,

Manorbier Castle, birthplace of the twelfth-century chronicler, Giraldus Cambrensis.

but was the subject of a 48-day siege by Cromwell in 1648, after its governor declared for the king, and was 'slighted' as a result.

Haverfordwest Castle stands sentinel on its natural hill overlooking the historic market town and the lowest fording point of the Western Cleddau, and withstood attacks from Llywelyn the Great and Owain Glyndwr. Another castle on an imposing site is **Cilgerran** (National Trust), high on its rocky promontory above the gorge of the River Teifi at its tidal limit near Cardigan, where coracles can often be seen in use. The romantic setting of the ruins of Cilgerran has inspired painters from Peter de Wint to the 'artist of light', J.M.W. Turner.

Manorbier Castle, former home of Giraldus Cambrensis, is another impressively-sited fortress, this time standing on a low promontory overlooking the beach and bay on the south coast. Built by the de Barri family, like so many others it was damaged during the Civil War, and a Victorian house was erected inside the inner ward in the 1880s. Other prominent castles in Pembrokeshire include those at **Roch**, **Tenby, Llawhaden** and **Picton**.

The outstanding ecclesiastical buildings in the National Park are undoubtedly **St David's Cathedral** and the **Bishop's Palace** in the tiny city of St Davids fully described in the Western section of this guide.

Other churches and chapels of interest include **St Non's Chapel**, the birthplace of the saint on the coast near St Davids; **St Govan's Chapel**, under the cliffs on the rocky south coast near Bosherston; **St Brynach's Church** and tenth-century **Cross,** at Nevern, and **St Issell's**, at Saundersfoot.

Museums and heritage centres abound in and around the National Park. They include the **Tudor Merchant's House,** at Tenby, a tiny but perfect late-fifteenth-century National Trust property which overlooks the little harbour. The **Tenby Museum and Art Gallery,** the **Haverfordwest Town Museum,** the **Milford Haven Museum** and the **Pembroke Dock Gun Tower Museum** all provide fascinating glimpses of the area's past, while the **Pembrokeshire Motor Museum**, near Haverfordwest, gives a more modern take on local transport.

There are many craftspeople and artists at work in the Pembrokeshire Coast National Park, and many have their own galleries and exhibitions during the season (more details in the products section and the National Park newspaper, *Coast to Coast*). Woollen mills producing home-spun materials also exist at **Melin Tregwynt and Solva Mill**.

If gardening is your passion, then a visit to the **Colby Woodland Gardens** at Amroth, run by the National Trust, is

The National Park Authority's award-winning Visitor Centre at St Davids.

St Catherine's Island, Tenby, crowned by a Victorian fort.

a worthwhile excursion. There is year-round interest in this eight-acre site, with fine displays of rhododendrons and azaleas and camellias rising from a carpet of bluebells in spring and early summer. There are many other gardens in the county which are open to visitors, along with small and large visitor attractions for all age groups.

Top Ten Historic Attractions

- Castell Henllys Iron Age Fort
- Carew Castle
- Pembroke Castle
- Manorbier Castle
- Tudor Merchant's House, Tenby
- St David's Cathedral and Bishop's Palace
- St Govan's Chapel
- Pentre Ifan, near Nevern
- Carreg Samson, near Mathry
- Colby Woodland Gardens

Tenby's imposing townscape overlooks the harbour.

13. Gazetteer of Towns and Villages

Abereiddi (SM 796310)

Once a thriving centre for slate quarrying, Abereiddi is now a quiet, attractive bay with only a few houses. Ruined quarrymen's cottages and a flooded quarry known as The Blue Lagoon can be seen from the Coast Path on the north side of the bay.

Amroth (SN 163072)

The former mining village of Amroth lies on the Pembrokeshire county boundary and marks the start of the 186-mile Pembrokeshire Coast National Trail. Famous for its submerged forest dating from 5000BC, tree stumps and trunks are exposed when exceptional tidal conditions lower the sand level. The village is divided into three parts – one at either end of the popular sand and pebble beach and the third around the Norman church of St Elidyr in the wooded valley behind.

Angle (SM 865030)

This peaceful village has a rich seafaring tradition and a reputation coloured by tales of smuggling and shipwrecks along the coast. The main street is backed by the medieval field strips of the Norman manor. The village lies beside Angle Bay, a shallow stretch of water with sheltered anchorage for fishing boats and pleasure craft.

Broad Haven (SM 861135)

Broad Haven began to develop as a seaside resort in Victorian times, when it featured bathing machines to preserve the bathers' modesty. It has been extensively developed in recent years, and the village is now an extremely popular holiday

The 186-mile Pembrokeshire Coast Path is usually started at the eastern end of Amroth beach.

destination. Its wide sandy beach and safe bathing make it ideal for families, as well as for sea anglers and surfers.

Bosherston (SR 966946)

A National Park car park provides easy access to the Bosherston Lakes – 80 acres (32 ha) of inter-connected fresh-water fish ponds managed as a National Nature Reserve by the National Trust. The profusion of white waterlilies is seen at its best in June. Bosherston's parish church of St Michael has two effigies and a cross in the churchyard which bears a carved image of the head of Christ.

Carew (Caeriw) (SN 045037)

Carew is the southernmost point of the Daugleddau section of the National Park and its main feature is the splendid castle dating from 1270. The castle is leased to the National Park Authority and open to the public, as is the restored 'French Mill', on the dam of the millpond. Carew Cheriton Church dates from the fourteenth century and contains tombs and effigies of the Carew family.

Dale (SM 812057)

Dale gives its name to the peninsula which shelters the entrance to Milford Haven. A lighthouse has stood on St Ann's Head since 1713 and there are spectacular cliff walks around the headland. Once a busy sea-trading and fishing village, Dale is now popular with water sports and sailing enthusiasts. The beach is sand and shingle and fine houses line the old quay wall.

Fishguard (Abergwaun) (SM 958370)

The picturesque harbour of Lower Fishguard was the setting for the 1971 film version of Dylan Thomas's *Under Milk Wood* and was once home to 50 coastal trading ships. The harbour, once important for fishing, is now used by leisure craft. Fishguard Fort was built in 1781 to protect the harbour from marauding privateers. However, it was on the wrong side of town when the abortive French invasion force of 1300 landed at Carregwastad Point near Llanwnda in 1797. Fishguard Square is the lively hub of the upper town, with varied shops and eateries. The long-established Fishguard summer music festival attracts an international audience.

Haverfordwest (Hwlffordd) (SM 955155)

Pembrokeshire's county town is dominated by the now ruined castle, said to date from the twelfth century, which today houses a museum. Steep, narrow streets reveal the town's medieval origins. There are three parish churches, of which the thirteenth-century St Mary's is the largest, and the ruins of a substantial priory. Standing at the highest navigable point of the Western Cleddau, Haverfordwest was once a busy port, and it remains an important market town. As well as being Pembrokeshire's administrative centre, Haverfordwest also has the county's biggest choice of shops. Behind the supermarkets and contemporary shop fronts are some fine buildings – examples of eighteenth-century, Regency and Victorian houses mingle with modern homes.

Dale is a very popular watersports centre.

Another view of Lower Fishguard.

Lawrenny (SN 018070)

Lawrenny is a pretty village lying inland in unspoilt, woodland surroundings and has numerous well-restored cottages. Nearby Lawrenny Quay, for many years a river port due to its position at the junction of Carew River and the Daugleddau, has become a yachting and holiday centre with a landing stage, boatyard and chandlery.

Little Haven (SM 857128)

Little Haven, once the centre of a mining area, is a picturesque village on a sheltered bay with a small beach. Anthracite from nearby pits was exported on coasting vessels, but the bay is now used only by pleasure boats. The village is now a busy holiday centre in summer, and there is a good variety of places to eat and drink. Nearby is the medieval church of Talbenny with spectacular views over St Brides Bay.

Manorbier (Maenorbyr) (SS 066978)

This historic and picturesque village was described as the 'most delectable spot in Wales' by Giraldus Cambrensis, the eminent churchman and historian born at Manorbier Castle in the twelfth century. The castle's mighty walls dominate the approach to the sheltered, sandy beach, once used by smugglers and now popular with summer visitors and surfers. Just above the beach on the eastern headland known as Priest's Nose is the King's Quoit, a Neolithic burial chamber capped with a massive block of local red sandstone. The parish church is also impressive; its nave dates to the twelfth century and its chapel, rebuilt in the fourteenth century, contains an effigy of a member of the de Barri family.

Marloes (SM 779083)

Once a village of lobster fishermen, Marloes still has close links with the sea and with the Pembrokeshire islands – boats for Skomer leave from nearby St Martin's Haven. Villagers used to gather leeches to sell to medical practitioners in Harley Street, London, for blood-letting. Nearby Marloes Sands are well-known among geologists for the colourful 400-million-year-old rocks exposed in the cliffs at the back of the beach. A geological feature is The Three Chimneys – originally near-horizontal rock layers up-ended by powerful earth movements.

Milford Haven (Aberdaugleddau) (SM 905058)

A Welsh town with a Norse name, Milford Haven was planned by an English landowner, Sir William Hamilton, settled by American whalers, and later peopled by deep sea fishermen and now by refinery workers. The town has strong associations with Admiral Nelson, lover of Sir William's wife Emma, who visited in 1802. With the arrival of the railway in 1863 came a period of prosperity – a large docks complex was built and became home to the sixth largest fishing fleet in Britain. The decline of the fishing industry in the late 1950s was offset by the growth of the oil industry. Part of the docks has been redeveloped to include a marina, and the town is home to the Torch Theatre, a museum, galleries and restaurants.

Narberth, a thriving market town at the heart of the county.

Narberth (Arberth) (SN 110146)

A market town at the heart of an agricultural area, Narberth is popular with artists and craftspeople. It has several workshops, galleries and antique shops, and a lively arts and music centre, the Queen's Hall. The town was the seat of the princes of Dyfed in the ancient collection of Welsh tales, *The Mabinogion*. Narberth Castle is said to have been built in 1246 on the site of an earlier castle of earth and timber. Businesses were opened to cater for the farmers, drovers and dealers who flocked to the town in their thousands for the weekly market, granted in 1688. The town is now noted for its food festival, literature festival and winter carnival.

Nevern (Nanhyfer) (SN 083401)

Nevern's Norman church is dedicated to the Celtic Saint Brynach, and in its churchyard, an imposing line of yew trees includes the 'Bleeding Yew', so-called because it drips blood-red sap. The splendid early-eleventh-century Nevern Cross stands nearby, from where – according to tradition – the cuckoo makes its first song on 7 April, St Brynach's feast day. Nevern Castle, an overgrown motte-and-bailey earthwork, tops a deep ravine above the church. The village boasts some fine Jacobean buildings.

Newgale (SM 850220)

Newgale has two miles of golden sands backed by a storm ridge of shingle, making it one of the most popular beaches in the National Park. The Brandy Brook at Newgale is the western end of the 'Landsker' – the social and linguistic line which divides Pembrokeshire. Tree stumps of a forest drowned in glacial times are occasionally exposed at very low tides.

Newport (Trefdraeth) (SN 057392)

Situated where the Preseli Hills meet the estuary of the River Nevern, Newport was the chief settlement of the lordship of Cemaes. The community grew up around the Norman castle, restored in 1859, when the gatehouse was converted into a private house. The street layout remains largely unchanged since medieval times. Fairs and markets were held in the town until the 1930s, and Newport became well known for seafarers and shipbuilders. More than 50 sailing vessels were built alongside the estuary and local merchants had shares in ships which traded along the Irish Sea and further afield. Newport has two beaches, Newport Parrog in the town and the long dune-backed expanse of Newport Sands, a short walk away at low tide.

Newgale – a long sandy beach at the western end of the Landsker.

Pembroke (Penfro) (SN 983015)
Pembroke has a long and interesting history, entwined with that of its magnificent castle – one of the first Norman strongholds in west Wales and later the birthplace of Henry VII. The town and castle are built on a ridge of limestone, and the town was well protected by a wall, parts of which still stand. Part of the natural river moat is now an attractive Mill Pond, home to water-fowl and otters. The castle was partially restored in 1880 but neglected until 1928, when it was leased to Pembroke Borough Council and conservation work was carried out. There are two Norman churches, while several buildings survive from the Benedictine period at nearby Monkton. The town has a good selection of shops, inns and restaurants and is a popular tourist base – the castle and quay host regular events through the summer.

Pembroke Dock (Doc Penfro) (SM 966034)
Pembroke Dock has a much shorter history than its neighbour. At the turn of the nineteenth century, only a hamlet called Pater Church existed on the south of the Haven. Following the expiry of the lease on the Milford Haven Dockyard, the Admiralty decided to transfer the dockyard across the waterway, leading to the birth of Pembroke Dock. Over 260 ships were built at the dockyard from 1814 to 1926, including Royal yachts. Until the early 1960s, Pembroke Dock was a garrison town, and the old dockyard was a famous flying-boat base in the Second World War. A ferry terminal has been constructed on part of the old dockyard.

Porthgain (SM 814327)
An atmospheric village dominated by the remains of its industrial past, it was an important slate-quarrying and exporting centre up to the 1930s, and later diversified into brick-making and stone quarrying. Above the tiny harbour stand the massive brick-built storage hoppers from which crushed stone was loaded into waiting ships, and the rows of quarry-workers' cottages also remain. The harbour is now used by lobster fishermen and pleasure boats, and the village is a popular place to eat and drink.

Rosebush (SN 074293)
At its peak, Rosebush Quarry employed some 100 men, many of whom lived in the 26 cottages which still form Rosebush Terrace. With the house-building boom of the 1860s, the slate quarry became the most productive in Pembrokeshire. Rosebush slates were used to roof the Houses of Parliament. When the market declined, Rosebush was promoted as a holiday resort, easily accessible by train thanks to the railway which opened in 1876 to link the quarry with the main London line. The quarry and the railway are now defunct, but Rosebush remains a popular hill-walking and pony-trekking centre.

St Davids (Ty Ddewi) (SM 753252)
The much-loved smallest city in Britain, St Davids has attracted visitors for more than a thousand years. In the sixth century, David, the patron saint of Wales, established a monastery here which became a central focus for early Christianity. The first cathedral was built on the site of St David's original monastery soon after the Norman Conquest. This was rebuilt, enlarged and embellished over the centuries to become the magnificent St David's Cathedral. Tucked away down a side street, it has been described as the finest church in Wales. The beautiful group of buildings in the Cathedral Close includes the cathedral, built partly of purple Cambrian rocks, the golden lichen-covered ruins of the thirteenth-century Bishop's Palace, and the restored College of St Mary. For centuries, what were said to be the bones of St David and St Justinian lay hidden, but were re-discovered in a nineteenth-century restoration and are now in the cathedral.

St Davids is a major centre for adventure sports, especially surfing and climbing. Boat trips to Ramsey Island leave from St

Cross Square, St Davids.

Saundersfoot.

Solva's lovely harbour.

A changing view on Tenby – the new lifeboat house alongside the century-old building which it replaced.

Justinian's, and nearby Whitesands Bay is the most popular of the handful of bays, beaches and inlets in the vicinity. The city is home to craft shops, galleries, cafés and restaurants, outdoor activity shops and an award-winning National Park Visitor Centre.

Saundersfoot (SN 137048)

Now a thriving seaside resort, Saundersfoot owes its development over the past two centuries to the local coalfield, though little evidence of its industrial past remains.

In 1829 a company was formed to construct a harbour to export high-quality anthracite coal, mined in Begelly, Kilgetty and Stepaside. The coal was transported by the narrow-gauge Saundersfoot Railway which operated until the closure of the last colliery in 1939, and the village has since been developed as a holiday resort. Today, the harbour is thronged with pleasure craft and the sandy, golden beaches are among the most popular along the whole coastline.

Solva (Solfach) (SM 805245)

Lower Solva was built out of sight of the sea and pirates, making its fjord-like inlet the safest harbour on this part of the coast. By 1811, more than 20 locally-owned vessels traded from the harbour, and the row of limekilns show that the production of lime to fertilise the fields was an important part of the trade. Solva was also noted for its woollen mills, one of which still operates at Middle Mill. The village is divided into two: Lower Solva lies at the head of the inlet, and is a mix of cottages, craft shops, galleries and pubs, while Upper Solva enjoys fine views of the harbour entrance and the Iron Age fort on the opposite headland. A small beach, the Gwadn, can be reached by a steep footpath over the headland into the next valley.

Stackpole (SR 984963)

Stackpole has had long links with the Earl of Cawdor. The eighteenth-century mansion of Stackpole Court is now demolished and the estate is owned by the National Trust. The nearby Stackpole Quay is an attractive little harbour famous for its shells and corals. South of the quay, the Coast Path leads to the beautiful sandy bays of Barafundle and Broad Haven, where sand dunes block the lower end of a valley which is taken up by the Bosherston Lakes (see entry for **Bosherston** p78).

Tenby (Dinbych-y-Pysgod) (SN 132004)

Tenby's four golden beaches, colourful harbour and ample accommodation make it one of the area's prime visitor destinations. The resident population of about 5000 is swelled by thousands during the holiday season, yet the town retains a charm and character which endear it to locals and visitors alike. The ruins of the castle stand on the promontory known as Castle Hill, and while only one of the five gateways into the Norman town remains, most of the ancient town walls are intact.

Ships traded with Bristol and as far afield as Spain and France from Tenby's scenic harbour. Today the harbour is used by pleasure craft and by boats to Caldey Island. The town's parish church of St Mary's dates from the thirteenth century and is the largest of the old parish churches in Wales. The Tudor Merchant's House near the harbour has been preserved by the National Trust to show how a Tenby merchant might have lived in the sixteenth century. Tenby Museum and Art Gallery is in the grounds of the castle and incorporates much of the castle's living quarters.

Trefin (Trevine) (SM 840325)

A large but typical coastal village near the inlets of Aberfelin and Abercastle. Its close links to the sea once gave it a reputation as a smuggling centre. Trefin inspired Crwys, a former Archdruid of Wales, and the village once belonged to the Bishop of St Davids. At Aberfelin, the ruin of a water-mill known as Melin Trefin is managed by the National Park Authority.

Porth Clais – the harbour for the cathedral city.

14. The National Park Today

Since 2004, the administrative centre for the Pembrokeshire Coast National Park Authority has been at Pembroke Dock. For an organisation whose duties include the protection of historic buildings, it is appropriate that the Authority is now located in a building which is both architecturally and historically important.

Llanion Park was completed in 1905 and was for over sixty years the headquarters of the resident Army garrison at Pembroke Dock. It is an imposing red brick building commanding fine views over the Haven Waterway. Although not in the National Park, it overlooks the lower reaches of the Haven which are part of the Park's area and close by is the boundary of the Daugleddau Sector – centred on the twin arms of the Cleddau rivers.

The Daugleddau is just one part of a very diverse and special landscape designated over half a century ago as one of Britain's first National Parks.

National Park status brought with it the highest measure of protection to an ever-changing coastline, rightly regarded as one of the finest in Europe, and also marked up the importance of the Preseli Hills, the famous offshore islands, and the Daugleddau.

The coastline is best seen from the spectacular Coast Path, a designated National Trail stretching 186 miles. Visitors spend the equivalent of one million days a year walking the path, contributing – at a conservative estimate – at least £14 million annually to the local economy.

The Authority works closely with many partner organisations, among them the Ministry of Defence and the National Trust, which are substantial land holders in the Park.

As a planning authority the National Park continues to handle an increasing number of applications annually – well over 600 at the latest count.

Fifteen members make up the National Park Authority, which has been a free-standing, special purpose authority since 1996. Ten of the members are county councillors appointed by Pembrokeshire County Council and five are appointed by the Welsh Assembly Government.

Seventy-five per cent of the Park's net budget is directly funded by the Welsh Assembly and the other quarter by Pembrokeshire County Council in the form of a levy. Additional funding comes from grants and income from various sources.

With an annual budget of around £5 million, the Authority's work is wide ranging and very varied – from running visitor centres to maintaining an intricate network of paths, and from controlling new building development to working with local schools.

More Information

Pembrokeshire Coast National Park Authority
Llanion Park
Pembroke Dock
Pembrokeshire SA72 6DY
Tel: 0845 345 7275

Friends of the Pembrokeshire National Park
PO Box 218
Haverfordwest
Pembrokeshire SA61 1WR

Council for National Parks
6/7 Barnard Mews
London SW11 1QU
Tel: 020 7924 4077

Wildlife Trust, South and West Wales
Welsh Wildlife Centre
Cilgerran
Cardigan SA43 2TB
Tel: 01239 621212

National Trust Office for Wales
Trinity Square
Llandudno LL30 2DE
Tel: 01492 860123

Cadw
Plas Carew
Unit 5/7 Cefn Coed
Parc Nantgarw CF15 7QQ
Tel: 01433 336000

Council for the Protection of Rural Wales
Ty Gwyn
31 High Street
Welshpool
Powys SY21 7YD
Tel: 01938 552525

Countryside Council for Wales
Plas Penrhos
Ffordd Penrhos
Bangor
Gwynedd LL57 2LQ
Tel: 01248 385500

Wales Tourist Board
Brunel House
2 Fitzalan Road
Cardiff CF2 1UY
Tel: 029 2047 5322

Maps
Ordnance Survey Explorer Maps (1:25,000)
OL35 North Pembrokeshire
OL36 South Pembrokeshire
Ordnance Survey Landranger Maps (1:50,000)
145 Cardigan & Mynydd Preseli
157 St Davids & Haverfordwest
158 Tenby & Pembroke